SECRET STRATEGIES TO EARN A LOT OF MONEY IN THE MULTI-LEVEL BUSINESS

DEVELOP YOUR SALES SKILLS, LEARN HOW TO SUCCEED IN A NETWORK MARKETING COMPANY

Gaston Echevarria

Table of Contents

Introduction: Multilevel Marketing

Multilevel marketing, or MLM, is a marketing strategy that creates a downline of distributors and a hierarchy of multiple levels of compensation. The sales force is compensated not only by their own sales but also by the sales of the people they help recruit. Companies, which have a large product base, often cannot employ an equivalent sales force; and believe they would be better off without the traditional approach. Therefore, they implement MLM to survive the competition of multinationals.

MLM is also known as network marketing because it uses a network of individual customers to hit other potential customers. In other words, each individual customer serves as a sales representative.

> ## *Multilevel Marketing vs. Pyramid Marketing*

People often confuse MLM with pyramid marketing; however, there is a very clear distinction between the two approaches: pyramid marketing is about getting your money and then using it to recruit other distributors; MLM, on the other hand, is about moving the product through a larger network of distributors so that the business can increase sales volume.

Another difference between MLM and pyramid marketing is that pyramid marketing requires that each level DOUBLE before creating a new level, so it's not fair to people who are in the lower levels and it's not ethical either. MLM, however, grants a commission based on the volume of product sold through its own sales efforts, as well as that of the downline organization.

Since MLM faces the risks of starting a business that has not been proven by unrecognized customers, people prefer to wait a coupe years before joining. Therefore, they also bear witness to the trajectory and reliability of the company.

> ## *Structure of multi-level marketing*

Multilevel marketing follows a significantly different structure than pyramid marketing: the network is divided into parts comprising a different number of people. Some parts of the network may be made up of people of lower rank because the initiator may not have been able to enroll more people; however, other parts may have flourished because a hard-working marketing genius has good resources. Therefore, MLM turns out to be a fairer approach to income generation.

> ➢ *Growth within multi-level marketing companies*

An MLM opportunity, with a wide network of contacts, brings with it greater growth prospects as members become more enthusiastic about introducing more people. In addition, those at the top of the network are encouraged to share their experiences with their subordinates. This is because improvements in the performance of new participants and subordinates will translate into greater benefits for older people.

Therefore, multi-level marketing companies can take advantage of great revenue-generating opportunities. The only key is to select one with a successful product or service; so that you prefer for yourself.

What Multilevel Marketing or MLM really is

Multilevel marketing is in fact a revolution in distribution. The evolution of multi-level marketing has fostered a change in business paradigm that has significantly changed the traditional ways of marketing and distributing a product to end users. Multilevel marketing has eliminated the need for additional stores, wholesalers, retailers and advertising budgets, making it one of the lowest cost marketing methods. Hence this new way of marketing has freed up a large amount of money that was previously consumed by huge advertising budgets and can now be used to develop better and innovative products.

- ### *Scope of multilevel marketing*

The multilevel marketing technique incorporates multiple levels of marketing that extend to masses of potential customers and this is what all companies really want to reach the maximum number of prospects. Especially with the advent of Internet marketing, the scope of MLM or network marketing has reached the apex. Companies in various industries such as health care products, beauty and skin care lines, cosmetics, and several others cannot really survive in the long run without implementing multi-level marketing strategies, especially in the course of their business.

Highlighting the scope of multi-level marketing, Michael L. Sheffield, CEO of Sheffield Research Network, a direct sales and MLM consulting firm, in his

February/March 1999 Direct Sales Journal, wrote an article entitled "Comp Plan Conversion: Direct Sales to MLM Compensation Plans" in which he argued that MLM has introduced a paradigm shift in the traditional direct selling business and with the Internet revolution the success of MLM companies has increased many times over. He also cited the statement produced by Neil Offen, president of the Direct Selling Association, that MLM had gone from 25 percent of the Direct Selling Association members in 1990 to 77.3 percent in 1999.

- ### *Multilevel Marketing Opportunities*

Multilevel marketing is a race of countless opportunities and prospects for growth in the economy. Today, multilevel marketing is not only considered one of the most profitable and efficient sources of marketing and distribution of its products and improvement of its sales, profits and business opportunities, but is also considered a source of employment generation in the economy. As more and more people move towards e-marketing and e-sales, MLM is creating an outbreak of employment opportunities and is considered a source of residual income for a number of people around the world, including students, unemployed, and women, especially housewives. Not only that, MLM offers a variety of benefits to companies to achieve maximum profits.

• *Understanding the MLM Model*

As mentioned above, MLM marketing is also known as network marketing and, as the name implies, has a multiple number of people (and/or networks) marketing a product to consumers. In very simple terms, in the framework of multi-level marketing, a company employs a sales representative (sometimes called a distributor, affiliate, or associate) who performs the following basic tasks.

First, get customers and generate sales.

Secondly, to generate, recruit and train other people as sales representatives to get customers or generate sales.

Let's discuss in detail how the multi-level marketing model works...

- ***Multilevel marketing model***

The following four-step model will demonstrate how a multi-level marketing model works:

Step I: Sales reps receive customers

Initially the MLM Company appoints a sales representative and/or distributor whose primary purpose is to sell the product or service to potential customers. The initial number of customers you have to get varies depending on the business plan and commission structure. But it's usually better to get as many customers as the person can retain effectively and make repeated sales to them. Also, if your company's payment structure is more rewarding to train people to get more customers than as an MLM salesperson, you should limit your efforts to get a few customers first at this stage and then focus on the next stage which is getting them trained to promote sales. This strategy is very appropriate for companies that pay you to "duplicate your identity".

Step II: Train and recruit a person as a sales representative:

After generating a few customers and making sales to them as normal direct marketing or direct sales does, the next job of a multi-level salesperson is to train a person to act as a sales representative and convince them to bring in more prospects and generate more sales for the company. This person would be called your downline. Here your role is that of a recruiter rather than that of a retailer or distributor.

Step III: You teach the representative how to train and recruit another person as a sales representative:

Once your sales representative gets enough customers at will and generates enough sales, it's time for you to train them to get a sales representative. Your work as a leader now has multiple dimensions, such as generating more sales, training staff to become a sales representative, and training the sales representative to train future staff as a sales representative. The focus of your efforts will again depend on your commission plan; you, as a seller, will concentrate your efforts where you can earn the highest commissions.

Step IV: Repeat the above steps to generate a string:

Once you recruit and train your sales representative to train more people and generate more customers, you can now recruit another sales representative and follow the same procedure by networking distributors within your downline. This is why it is called multi-level or network marketing and therefore companies through MLM tactics can not only generate reliable customers, but they can also bring their products and/or services to masses of people with minimal costs and in a relatively shorter period of time compared to traditional marketing methods.

The above procedure explains the MLM model well, but is it always easier to obtain as it appears? Or how is it possible for a company to promote MLM marketing? A well-designed compensation plan is the only answer to the above questions. In our next chapter we will discuss guidelines for developing an effective compensation plan.

Practical advice

As mentioned above, multi-level marketing is simply a business model for moving products and services from production to consumer using a network of independent distributors with a multi-level commission payment plan. Since distributors can recruit other distributors and set up teams to work together, the payment plan is also a bit complex. In any MLM company the basic key to driving the MLM marketing force in the direction required to produce the best results is the compensation plan. Commission plans or compensation plans are the way MLM companies reward a distributor's production that drives the distribution channel to maximize profits.

➢ *Basic Compensation Strategy*

It is important to note that each company is different and each has different commission plans, some of which also seem complex or complicated. However, the underlying elimination strategy has the following basic components.

Retail sales commission: As the name implies, the retail commission is the commission assigned to motivate the seller to generate sales. The commission paid to a seller for the number of sales he makes to his customers.

Sponsor Commission: The next component of an MLM compensation plan is the commission paid to a seller for sales generated by their downline, requiring the seller to focus on persuading and generating other sales representatives for the sales promotion. Companies that want to expand their marketing and distribution efforts usually pay better commissions to motivate their salesperson to bring more sales representatives to the company.

Training Commission: Few companies also pay their salespeople to train sales representatives. These salespeople basically act as leaders and have the experience, knowledge and skills to train new staff.

In addition to the above components it is also important to mention that MLM is all about leveraged revenue which is a sales representative who not only earns commissions on their own sales, but also earns commissions on sales generated by people they have introduced, trained and recruited as sales representatives. It is also imperative that marketers beware of tactics that are sometimes not ethically used by a few MLM companies when developing complex compensation plans. In the following chapters we will discuss MLM scams and frauds and the means to prevent them.

✓ *How to Find a Good MLM Business*

Although the Multilevel Marketing business has very good opportunities and prospects for growth and success, however, the static reveals that most people who enter this company face an obstacle. A study reveals that almost eighty-five percent of MLM businesses fail in the first eighteen months. Therefore, for a person it is essentially vital to start this business prudently. Here are some guidelines to follow:

Step *I*: RESEARCH THE COMPANY

It is critical to the success of a marketer to join a company that is solid and viable to enter as a multi-level marketer. Here are some points to consider:

Start with a company with a lot of experience:

In order to get into multi-level marketing, it is usually wise to start with an experienced company that has been in business for at least three years or more. The reason is that the company itself has passed the initial survival phase and must now be in the growth phase increasing its chances of success as a marketer.

Opt for a Public Limited Company:

Well-known and established corporations are not only safer to enter, but also have easy and high-level access to information about the background of the company, its people, and its commercial and financial strength. It is also recommended to compare the salary or commission with the average sales of the company that will tell you if it is a good place to start.

Select a member of a business office:

It is always ideal to join a company that is a member of a business office or registered with the Direct Selling Association. This not only guarantees the reliability of the company, but it can also present its complaints to these organizations regarding any misconduct on the part of the company.

✓ ***Investigate the company's history:***

Essentially important is to look at the company, to see how it does business. Is it for ethical reasons? Check his record. Find out if you have a stable track record and identify if the company's values match yours. It is essentially important for the long-term presence in the multi-level marketing industry.

Step II: RESEARCH THE PRODUCT:

Along with identifying a solid company, it is also very important to know the product to be marketed. Remember that your success as a multi-level seller ultimately depends on the sales of the product you are offering. Here are some questions to investigate:

✓ *Is the product marketable?*

As a seller it is important to buy a product that is highly marketable and has solid qualities and characteristics through which you can promote sales. Also to sell products it is necessary to know their characteristics. Sometimes it is essentially important to research and have enough knowledge to commercialize your self-esteem. For example, if you are selling some computer software, you should have a good knowledge of the technology. Therefore, before buying a business, a marketer must evaluate these issues.

✓ *Do you like the product?*

If you like the product, it will be easier for you to market it and therefore you can also convince others to become sales representatives. Remember that multilevel marketing is more word-of-mouth, when you like yourself you feel safer because you know the product is good and you are not making false promises.

✓ *Is it reasonably priced?*

Naive sellers often ignore the importance of price, which is one of the reasons for their failure in the field. It is essentially important to ensure that your product is well priced and has excessive qualities or is comparatively cheaper than other brands available on the market, otherwise it will be almost impossible for a seller to generate enough sales. Also some companies offer discounts on a certain number of sales, you should identify the associated discounts to improve your profits.

✓ *Is the product consumable?*

To generate more commissions, try to select consumer products, as this increases the chances of repeating sales. In addition, if your customer likes the product, you can retain it for the long term and therefore convince him to act as a sales representative, which will ultimately increase our future profits.

✓ *Is there a demand for the product?*

Never select products that are obsolete or excessively available at the point of sale. If your products do not have enough demand, you would be wasting time and effort for nothing.

Step III: RESEARCH THE COMPENSATION PLAN:

The next crucial step is to understand the compensation plan well. As most of the time a multi-level vendor is providing a dual service; one as a vendor and the other as a recruiter, therefore your commission and compensation depends on both. This is why it is important to understand the company's compensation policies well in advance. Here are some tips:

✓ *Is your compensation based on sales or recruitment?*

Remember that it is illegal to pay commissions on the number of recruits. Therefore, you must identify the compensation plan. This will help you concentrate your efforts.

Identify hidden costs:

Some companies require a down payment or membership fee to register as a seller or sales representative on behalf of the companies. Identify if you are going to generate

enough commissions to cover your initial money paid. Also if the investment is relatively high, be careful as some fraudulent companies ask to pay large sums initially. Always refrain from joining them.

✓ **Do you have a target to reach?**

You must find your goals, for example, how many members you have to recruit. Some companies require you to enroll a certain number of people in a certain period of time before receiving payment. Not only that few companies require you to cross the target sales level before paying you. This can cause problems for new and naive salespeople.

In addition to the above, there are also other important points that guarantee your success as a multi-level seller. These are the ones:

Vendor training:

Some companies offer training to their MLM sales representatives and salespeople on product features and company profile. Good companies also train their staff to improve their marketing skills. It is best to select such a company, especially if you are new to the multilevel marketing industry.

Active participation:

Some companies also offer a discussion forum where you can interact with other members. It's good for you, because in the course of your work some questions may arise to which you need answers and you want to receive suggestions from other people in the same company who can help you resolve your doubts and give you the right answers you need.

Accept the current member's recommendation:

Always contact someone who is already a member of MLM. Ask them for their recommendations about the company and their views on how the MLM system works in the company.

Beware of scams:

There are a number of false companies and false claims. Be careful with them. In the following chapters we will discuss in detail MLM scams, which will help protect you from getting into fake companies.

In a nutshell, a good company is made up of people who are committed to products that really help improve people's lives, who see their distributors as their assets and have promising compensation plans that pay well for efforts, who train their people and who are always there to help their people. Therefore, if you follow the above steps, you will be able to select a good MLM company that will guarantee you success as a multi-level marketer.

Multilevel marketing versus traditional businesses

Multilevel marketing advocates describe MLM as the most efficient and effective means of marketing and generating contacts and sales for your business. But traditional marketing companies are reluctant to adopt new network marketing strategies to run their business. In addition, most people don't even exactly understand the differences between the two strategies. This is why we have dedicated this chapter to exploring the difference between multi-level marketing and traditional marketing strategies.

Let's explore the main differences:

- ## **Difference between MLM and Traditional Marketing**

The most significant difference between MLM and traditional marketing is the role of the marketer. In multi-level marketing, an individual is initially hired as a sales representative who must market the company and its products and/or services and generate sales, which is quite similar to any traditional marketing business. However, on the other hand, within the framework of multi-level marketing, you are also required to identify and recruit additional sales representatives as your downline. The new sales representative may in turn appoint another person as the company's sales representative or marketer.

Under MLM one salesperson has the authority to get customers and recruits and trains another salesperson to get customers. However, in a traditional marketing company, a sales manager and/or sales representatives are hired by the company itself.

Under MLM an unlimited number of sales reps can be hired regardless of whether they generate enough sales or not, however, under a non-MLM company sales reps are hired based on the company's financial resources. A new sales manager is also hired only when the existing manager is overwhelmed.

In an MLM company the structure of the distribution network expands vertically, however in a traditional marketing company there is generally a horizontal expansion.

MLM sellers often receive commissions, i.e. their compensation is usually based on the number of sales made by them or by people in their downline. This is why MLM enjoys rapid expansion, as salespeople can recruit as many sales reps as they wish and the company does not have to worry about fixed salaries. However, in traditional marketing, sales managers or representatives are often paid fixed salaries.

In addition, MLM companies do not usually require high establishment costs compared to traditional companies that require large investments to establish an entire marketing and distribution channel.

One of the other main features of multi-level marketing is that parent companies make a lot of money. MLM's sales force is so vast that even if no promoter sells at high levels, but the group as a whole sells at a very high level, the company would still enjoy the benefits. However, under the traditional system, if a manager is not functioning well, the company's sales are negatively affected.

Under MLM, those with high performance earn a lot and reach the top, while the rest (those with low performance) cannot survive and leave the market on their own. The MLM company, like any other traditional company, does not have to worry about going through the tedious procedures of appraisals, hiring and firing, and so on.

Therefore, the above differences clearly manifest the advantages associated with multi-level marketing over traditional marketing methods, since MLM is not only the most flexible form of marketing, but also, due to its network characteristic, has the tendency to expand rapidly in the market and, if effectively targeted, can make huge profits for the company. Not only can people who can join the marketing team under MLM work at any time and reap the benefits not only on the sales they make, but also on the sales made by the representatives they recruit. Therefore, MLM has the characteristics of enjoying leveraged revenues and greater market penetration.

✓ *You must improve your skills as a salesperson*

It is essential for a salesperson to understand that, no matter how large the company they select and how demanding the products, what should not be forgotten is that multi-level marketing requires a lot of work and commitment. It is not possible to make large sums of money by just signing up once and then sitting around waiting for the money to arrive. You need to constantly train and update yourself and improve your efforts to ensure long-term profits and maximize profits. Here are some tips to help you improve your skills as a multi-level salesperson.

Managing your downline:

Remember that your downline is your asset and a source of income. Therefore, it is important to manage your downline properly and continue to motivate your downline to produce maximum results and generate maximum sales.

Understand different people:

It is important for a salesperson to understand that he or she is dealing with a number of people at a time, most of them from different backgrounds. It is essential for him to train each of them appropriately as each may require a different set of information and skills to improve their efficiency. Also in order to convince people to act as a sales representative, you as a salesperson must persuade them according to their needs and level.

Learn to accept rejection:

Multi-level marketing has a high rejection rate, so it is important to maintain a positive attitude and accept taking a "NO".

Stay focused and be persistent:

Some people tend to lose interest quickly if they think their plans aren't working perfectly. A multi-level marketer should avoid this, as it requires persistence and focused efforts to achieve success.

Conduct constant research:

Once again, your success as a seller depends largely on the company and the product you select. It is therefore imperative to investigate well before entering the company.

Train and update yourself constantly:

Try to pick up companies that offer constant training to their salespeople, this will help you keep your auto update. If you understand the latest trends, technologies and product features, you will be in a better position to persuade customers, generate sales and lead your downline.

Improve your communication skills:

Effective communication and sales skills are key to each salesperson's success; therefore, a multi-level salesperson must constantly improve his or her communication skills.

Talk for talk... reliability:

To achieve repeat sales, it is necessary to provide reliable information. Therefore, you should be responsible for marketing your product and avoid unethical ways of generating sales and prospects.

Successful Multilevel Companies

MLM Business Essentials

Thousands of MLM companies are operating in the world today, but most of them disappear over time. New companies keep coming in and out of the market. Only large companies can maintain a long-term existence. It is essentially important to find out which companies are successful in MLM? What are their characteristics? How a company can ensure the success of its MLM strategies. These are some of the highlights of a high-performance multi-level marketing company.

✓ *Unique product:*

No matter how effective your sales or marketing strategy and how good your sales force is, nothing works if your offer isn't worth it. A unique and well-developed product that truly satisfies the customer's needs is a necessity. Without a quality product that is unique in the market, you cannot survive in the market, no matter how big you are.

✓ *Stability:*

The word stability often denotes longevity and long-term endurance. A well-established company has the opportunity to retain short-term economic shocks in demand and prices. Companies with coherent management plans and policies and defined long-term objectives also demonstrate long-term stability and persistence. If key decisions and decision-makers have changed frequently throughout the company's history, their stability is questionable.

✓ *Financial strength:*

Stability and financial soundness is another component of stability. Before entering MLM, a company must identify whether it has adequate resources and funds to comply with distributor compensation. Companies must also identify whether it would be profitable to implement network marketing and whether the expected benefits outweigh the associated costs.

✓ *Training and support for members*

The most important characteristic of a well performing multi-level marketing company is the quality of its training and support to distributors or affiliates.

Companies that see their distributors as active always focus on educating and training their people not only to hone their skills but also to enable them to keep up with any changes or new trends in the multilevel marketing industry. These companies offer ongoing training to their sales teams through webinars, chat rooms and videoconferences. In addition, successful companies offer different channels to their distributors to resolve questions and concerns, such as live chat rooms, resource libraries, informative and interactive websites, and distributor support hotlines.

✓ *Tools for the creation of companies*

It is important to remember that successful salespeople are imperative to a company's success. This is why high-performance multi-level marketing companies often provide their distributors with a variety of effective business creation tools. Various useful tools such as electronic cards, journals, calendars, customer relationship management systems, samples, testers, auto responders and various other online resources are provided to your distributors.

✓ *Compensation Plan*

An effective compensation plan is again a necessity for the success of multi-level marketing. An effective MLM marketing company knows the importance of its distribution force and offers its distributors a generous and balanced compensation plan. It is also important that whatever compensation model the company uses, the plan is simple, straightforward and easy to understand, and that it rewards its distributors or affiliates with progressive bonus levels. To motivate them to increase their efforts to increase sales volume and recruit more qualified prospects.

Therefore, these are the basic characteristics that ensure the survival and success of a multi-level marketing company, these few characteristics should guide how to ensure the success of multi-level marketing.

Is Multilevel Marketing Legal?

Multilevel marketing is a relatively new and complex marketing concept, although it has been practiced for years in one form or another by many companies, but the vast majority of people confuse it with pyramid schemes and question the legality of multilevel marketing. Now the question is, is MLM legal? Here's the answer: Yes, it's legal.

Until 1979, multilevel marketing was usually considered a scam or illegal because it was never proven and adjudicated in court. In 1975, Amyway Corporation was charged and sued by the U.S. Federal Trade Commission for operating as an illegal pyramid scheme and after four years of litigation, Amyway won the case and the court ruled out that the company's multi-level marketing program was a legitimate business and not an illegal pyramid scheme. Therefore, it is now quite clear that multi-level marketing is legal and not a scam.

For now it is clear that multilevel marketing is legal and should not be thought twice. However, companies that carry out multi-level marketing programs must strictly develop strategies that fall under the definition of multi-level marketing, as there is a fine line between multi-level marketing and pyramid marketing that is illegal. Also due to the complexity of commission structures, companies sometimes develop, if not illegal but unethical strategies that are not beneficial to communities and the general public.

However, in order to legally enter the category of multi-level marketing, in addition to using common sense, the following guidelines of the United States Federal Trade Commission (FTC) must be followed:

Never enter into any plan that promises commissions for recruiting additional distributors. It is constituted under an illegal pyramid scheme. Your compensation must be linked to actual sales made by you or your downline, not to the number of recruits.

Plans that ask new distributors to make an advance payment or buy expensive inventory are often skeptical, so it is essential to be cautious with them. These plans can collapse quickly and can also be finely disguised pyramid schemes.

Also, plans that claim that you will earn more money by increasing your downline are unrealistic. You are paid commissions on the sales made by the people you recruit, not just by hiring more and more representatives. So be careful with them.

Watch the shillings. False or overprojected references used by companies to attract you are unrealistic, so be careful.

Remember, you don't sell miracles. Therefore, the commitment to companies that claim to sell miraculous products. Also remember that under FTC guidelines, a distributor or salesperson is ethically responsible for the promises he or she made. So don't promise what you can't deliver.

Never enter into a contract in a "Now or Never" high pressure situation. These are all unethical tactics practiced by companies to trap you. Always take your time and take the advice of friends and other professionals such as accountants, lawyers, etc. to evaluate the feasibility of the project.

In addition to the above guidelines, the FTC also requires the multi-level marketing company to derive at least 70% of its revenue from retail sales to nondealers. If this criterion is not met, the courts have concluded that in several cases the MLM company is in the business of unceasingly recruiting distributors who recruit distributors, which may turn these companies into pyramid schemes, not into sales and distribution companies.

Therefore, the above guidelines are important in identifying whether the MLM Company falls within the legal definition of doing business. But that's not all; apart from being legal, it's essentially important for the multi-level marketing company to use ethical standards and procedures to generate its business and profits. Later in this text we will highlight the general scams and unethical practices that are often practiced by few MLM companies to deceive their people and ways to avoid them.

Possible scams and how to avoid them

As mentioned above, the success of MLM depends to a large extent on the increase in the number of sales through sales representatives. Sometimes companies, in order to attract people, use false claims. This is one of the main reasons many people fear MLM is because they believe they are going to be swindled. If you search the web you will find many examples of companies that make false claims and MLM scams. Here are some examples of how companies use unethical practices to deceive people:

Offer money-back guarantee schemes

Offer miracles instead of real products

Ask new distributors to pay in advance

Promises to give people in the ranks once they sign up with them

Sometimes MLM companies don't even exist in reality, they just create fake websites to trap individuals.

Require you to buy a certain percentage of your product initially, which you may not be able to sell and therefore incur losses.

Promising you unreasonably high commissions on your sales.

Aside from them, many MLM companies

tactically plan their commission scheme that actually takes money away from vendors or people working on the network. Naive salespeople usually don't understand that they are being swindled and even after putting in a hundred percent of their efforts and generating enough customers, they don't achieve the unrealistic goals of the companies and can't get anything out of their efforts. This is why it is always essential that a salesperson think carefully and investigate properly before entering the MLM company and stay away from companies that apply unethical tactics to generate profits.

Here are some tips for avoiding scams.

➢ *Tips for Avoiding Multilevel Marketing Scams:*

Investigate the company and its

management. For example, if you have no access to the company, no phone numbers, no addresses, no contact persons, then these are the signs that you are being swindled.

Read the policy and procedures before joining. Also take the advice of some professionals before signing any agreement.

Avoid lead generation systems that rely on friends and family.

We'll understand the compensation plan. Also make sure that you are being compensated for the sales you and your downline generate and not for the number of people you recruit, since the latter is an illegal pyramid scheme.

Check to see if support is available for the top line. Identify whether the company invests funds and resources in the training of its distributors. Only good and reliable companies will invest in the training of their personnel.

If the multi-level marketing company is asking for several hundred or thousands to join in advance, there may be chances of being swindled.

Always remember that MLM's success takes time and hard work, never join companies that promise overnight profits.

By following the above tips, a naive salesperson can reduce the chances of being swindled and therefore focus their efforts on a reliable and realistic MLM business.

Multilevel Online Marketing Opportunities

So far our discussion has been based on an understanding of the fundamentals of multi-level marketing and one thing that is obvious throughout our discussion is that each multi-level marketing company aims to reach more and more prospects and generate more and more sales. Now just think for a moment about the current era, which is the best possible means to reach the maximum number of prospects by investing the minimum amount of time and effort. The answer is very simple: `Internet'. By connecting online, MLM companies can transform their business into success and reach billions of customers by incorporating multi-level online marketing strategies. The best multi-level marketing companies execute several online marketing strategies in order to generate more and more business opportunities and then concentrate their marketing efforts on the opportunities to generate sales.

Guidelines for Efficient Multilevel Online Marketing

Let's explore some guidelines to make your online MLM business a success;

> ➢ **Create your website:**

The first and most important step in securing your online presence is to create your website. Every online multilevel marketing system starts with a website.

> ➢ *Attract visitors:*

No matter how good your company, your product or your website is, it's worthless if nobody knows it? Therefore, the next step is to attract traffic to your website. Now the question is how to do that. The answer is to announce yourself. This can be done through the incorporation of various online marketing strategies, such as through article marketing, viral marketing, blogging, video marketing, social marketing, and so on.

marketing, sponsored ads such as pay-per-click etc. To generate maximum traffic to your website it is essentially important to use effective keywords and develop content and tactics that maximize your search engine rankings. All of these procedures, if used efficiently, can attract billions of visitors to your website.

> ***Generate potential clients:***

Once you get traffic to your website it is now the stage where you get contact information to build lists of interested prospects. Generating leads and creating lists is the most important step. Later in this text we will explore in detail the ways in which leads can be generated. You can do this through compression pages, opt-in email pages, pop-ups, etc. Therefore, in this way you can get information about the person who is interested in your company and your product and you can buy your product in the future.

> **Building relationships:**

Once a lead is generated, it's time to establish a relationship with the prospect and develop trust and persuade them to buy the product. Keeping in touch with your prospect is crucial. This can be done through an auto responder, where you send a predefined set of emails to the prospect to create credibility and trust.

> ## *Generate sales:*

Once you've done that, you can convince your potential customer to buy your product and turn lead into a customer. Remember to keep in touch with your customer so that you can not only make repeat sales, but also convince them to join your team and eventually recruit them as sales representatives.

By following the guidelines above, you, as a salesperson, can reap maximum benefits and lead to success. However, it is essentially important for a multi-level vendor to develop a long-term relationship with their customers, as it is the key to their long-term survival in the MLM industry. In the next chapter we will explore the importance of relationship building.

The importance of relationships

For every business the key to success is building relationships with its customers. This is also true for any multi-level marketing business, in fact, the importance of building a relationship increases twice in multi-level marketing, as you as a salesperson not only have to retain your customers to generate repeat sales, but also build trust with them so that you can convince them to join your team as a salesperson and as a future sales representative. So how do you build relationships online? Here are the basic tips you need to follow to build online relationships.

Add value to your customers:

One of the best ways to retain your customers is to consistently provide value to them. In multi-level marketing, one of the best ways to add value to your potential customers is to provide them with the best product. When your product satisfies customers, it means that you have fulfilled the promises made to them and therefore develop your credibility and people trust you and will return to you repeatedly.

This is it? No, remember that we are talking about MLM marketing, where your profits are based on the sales made by your downline. Therefore, for a multi-level salesperson it is equally important to build healthy and lasting relationships with people in their downlines. Your low lines are your assets. Always try to train, help and meet your needs and always be there to solve your problems and problems. In this way, you can not only increase your own revenues, but you can also increase your company's profits.

Mark yourself:

As many people are doing multi-level marketing business online and in order to differentiate themselves from their competitors and prove themselves, it is essential that you brand yourself. The best way to do this is to create your own website or blog that tells people about you. When you do, you increase your credibility and win over your competitors.

Stay in touch:

A very common mistake that most MLM salespeople make is to leave customers once they make sales. Don't ever do that. It is very important to keep in touch with the customer, asking him how he found the product, what else he wants in the product. These tactics will help you retain your customers for the long term and ensure repeat sales.

Be positive:

Few traders get angry quickly because of fluctuations in market demand. It is important as a leader to remain positive and persistent, even if there are not enough sales. The reason behind whether your loose hopes can't motivate people in your downline, therefore, always stay positive and focused.

➢ *Generation of potential customers*

Throughout our discussion within this text we have highlighted that a multi-level marketer has to achieve two basic objectives. One is to sell the products or services of the parent company and the other is to encourage the customer to also become an independent distributor. Both objectives require actions that require the creation of maximum business prospects, also known as "business leads".

There are several ways to generate potential customers. Typically, a salesperson generates their own leads through referrals from friends, family and acquaintances. But is that enough? Therefore, the seller has to use various tools such as holding events or trade fairs, distributing brochures, others may include conducting research or even the seller may simply buy a list of construction companies from lists or other relevant sources.

Multi-level online sellers also use various

tactics to generate leads. This can be done through compression pages, opt-in email pages, pop-ups, etc. These are basically common ways to collect information from a visitor, for example, through the compression page you provide a piece of information in the form of an article or video clip for the customer and then ask the customer to leave their contact details (usually email, postal address, and other contact information) if they need more details. This way you will be able to get information about the person who can buy your product in the future. Therefore, if you have an online existence, you are in a position to generate masses of business contacts, which are basically your potential customers. Once you get them, it will help you to maintain a long-term relationship with them and you will be able to approach them to offer yourself, your offers and your services.

Therefore, a multi-level marketer must generate as many contacts as he can, which is crucial not only for his existence but also for the survival of the company.

➢ *Multilevel Marketing Performance Measurement*

An integral part of analyzing the success of a multi-level marketing campaign is measuring the performance of the multi-level marketing team. You need to identify key performance indicators that have a significant impact on your company's profitability. These key indicators are basically checkpoints that help you monitor the progress of your multi-level marketing team and its effects on your business. Due to the very complex nature of the network marketing scenario and generally complicated compensation plans, few companies sometimes ignore evaluating their team's performance and overall impact on the business. But is it okay or is it a big mistake? Only a madman would say he has a right.

The performance of a multi-tier team has a vital impact on your business and it is crucial to evaluate the performance as it will help you formulate your future business strategies and multi-tier marketing plan. Invest more in areas that are promising and reduce efforts where there is not much potential. But the question is how do you measure your team's performance? How can you provide useful data for planning future business strategy? What are the key performance indicators?

To assess performance it is essential to identify key performance indicators. For example, identify whether your team has achieved the goals assigned to it, the number of sales made by your team, the number of key recruits you get, performing a cost-benefit analysis, the number of repeat sales or repeat customers, the increase in sales, the level of satisfaction of your team, the level of satisfaction of your customers, and so on. Once you do, you can use these results to develop future business policies. Measurement of key performance indicators is therefore a well-recognised process and is practised by almost all large companies to use as a basis for formulating future strategies.

Another important point to bear in mind is the evaluation of your business objectives. Some companies set unrealistic targets that are very difficult to achieve. To evaluate actual performance it is also essential to evaluate your compensation plan. For example, if distributor retention is very low, rather than penalizing your team, you should re-evaluate your commission plan and identify why your team cannot produce effective results. Also note the forces that are not in control of your vendors, e.g. an economic downturn, short drop demand, etc. Therefore, in order to ensure longevity, MLM companies must constantly evaluate the performance of their equipment and take steps to correct any holes in the loop.

Advantages of multi-level marketing

Multilevel marketing offers a variety of benefits. Listed below are some advantages associated with the MLM business:

- ### *Minimum entry barriers:*

Multilevel marketing like any other online marketing is an egalitarian industry that you can enter and has no entry requirement for pain. Also to start your career as a multi-level salesperson and to start an MLM business professionally you don't need to be highly qualified, i.e. you can enter this business without the need for a degree or any particular experience.

- *Financial flexibility:*

Compared to other businesses, the MLM business has relatively low establishment costs. Although actual costs vary substantially with the type of compensation plan you offer, for example, few companies require a substantial monthly investment in products or services or few require some additional charges such as registration, etc. to join them as your sales representative or salesperson.

- *It demands focused efforts:*

The approach of an MLM salesperson is only to market the product that is you have to concentrate your efforts on generating sales and sales representatives. Everything else is done by the company itself, i.e. you are only marketing a product that has already been manufactured, and when you make a sale you don't have to worry about anything else, such as sending the product to the customer, etc.

- *Flexible schedule:*

You can manage your business any time you want. You have the flexibility to choose your work schedule. You can work part-time, full-time, in the evenings, from home or elsewhere. In addition, you don't need a suitable office or corporate area from which to work.

- *MLM offers leveraged income:*

One of the greatest advantages in an MLM business is that you basically put initial efforts into training and generating an effective sales representative and developing an efficient downline. Once you do, you can reap the profits for the rest of your life. Because you are generally earning compensation or commission on sales generated by you, as well as your downline, and the more efficient and hardworking your downline, the more money you can earn. This is why MLM is usually seen as a source of leveraged income, i.e., you receive a continuous income from a single initial effort.

- ***Pre-existing systems***

As an MLM vendor you do not need to develop systems to recruit, develop and train your staff. These are handled by the company you represent. All you have to do is reach out to people to market your product and generate sales and convince them to act as future sales representatives.

- **Personal growth and development:**

MLM marketing is also seen as an extensive source of personal growth and vendor development. Over time, not only do you achieve professional sales qualities, but MLM helps you increase your public relations and improve your marketing and leadership qualities.

> **Disadvantages of multi-level marketing**

Having discussed the advantages, let's now explore the darker side that are the disadvantages of multi-level marketing. Here's the list:

- **Complex Compensation Plans:**

It is important to note that compensation or commission plans are not usually as simple as they seem. Most of the time companies to keep MLM financially viable set a set of objectives based on sales, performance-based or standards-based and are only paid once these objectives are achieved. For example, few companies pay only if you hire a specific number of representatives to generate future sales; if you don't, you won't get anything from your sales.

- **Financial commitment:**

Few companies trap marketing professionals by asking them for a series of hidden charges in the form of registration fees, training fees or even, on occasion, charge for the marketing material or tools they provide (e.g. CDs, brokers, manuals, etc.) to marketing professionals to provide training on the product and its characteristics, as well as on the company. Most of the time, you will need to commit to purchasing a certain volume of product each month in order to remain eligible to participate in the program. This makes it difficult for you to remain profitable and hampers your long-term existence in the industry.

- ### *It requires broad motivation:*

Remember that MLM is about leveraged income. You can only survive when you earn money from your own sales plus the sales generated through your downline. Therefore, it is vitally important to keep your downline motivated and focused. It is also necessary to train and recruit more and more people to generate more income. Therefore, MLM requires continuous effort and hard work for future survival.

- ***Severe competition:***

As the MLM business does not require any professional title or skill, and moreover has relatively no barriers of initiation or entry, it fosters severe competition. Anyone can enter the market and take away your prospects. This is why to ensure longevity, a serious MLM salesperson has to work really hard as there are many others out there willing to work with their sponsors.

The Business Perspective

There is so much hype everywhere about the success of MLM and the financial and other rewards associated with employing a successful MLM campaign. But what are the statistics? What are the real facts? If you do your research you will find that although several companies associate their success stories to MLM. Big giants like Avon, Amyway, Mary Kay and many others have great MLM teams that are an advantage for them. But it is also true that almost seventy or eighty percent of companies entering the field for the first time encounter failures and losses. Why is that? Where are things going wrong? Here are some areas that require proper consideration:

- **_Reasons for MLM failures_**

Let's find out some reasons for MLM failures from a company's perspective:

- **_Selecting the wrong people:_**

One of the biggest pitfalls is the selection of the wrong people. In order to maximize their commissions, MLM promoters often select anyone when recruiting individuals to be part of their downline. People who are not really serious and if they can't make enough commissions, portray a bad image of the company everywhere. This is dangerous for the future growth of a company. Other people may be reluctant to join the company and/or buy the product.

- *Commitment to research and development:*

It is also essential that companies remember that MLM is an integral part of their business strategy. Few companies focus all their efforts on MLM and forget the rest. This is where things go wrong. With excellent marketing efforts it is also crucial to invest in research

and the development and production of a unique product with sound characteristics. No matter how good your marketing and distribution network is, without a promising product, everything else is useless.

- *Commission plans inflated:*

Some companies, in order to attract

more and more people and to stay ahead of the competition, offer commission plans and prices for unrealistic or over-inflated products and promise wealth overnight. Avoid doing that, first, because it could soon collapse financially; second, it can be seen as a scam and people are reluctant to join you.

• *Inability to understand market supply and demand:*

In the greed to expand market penetration and reach millions of people, the biggest mistake some companies make is to forget the basic economy. It is essential to assess market demand and product supply. Companies may spend huge sums of money on MLM, but what they don't realize is the economic scenario. Also the price you set is a determinant of demand and supply, especially if the product you offer is not too different from what is already available everywhere in the market. It is therefore essential to assess all these factors before investing blindly in MLM.

• *Use of unethical practices:*

The most dangerous movement that can damage a company's image is the implementation of unethical practices to generate short-term profits. Practices such as making false promises about product attributes, charging a high upfront fee or requiring a large initial investment from new people to join your distribution team, forcing them to buy a large number of products that are really impossible to sell, can make you profit in the short term but damage your image and existence in the long term.

It is true that MLM promises large sums

of money, but it is essential to realize that there are no miracles and that you must be prudent and vigilant in developing MLM strategies and must use legitimate and ethical tactics, otherwise it will collapse.

➢ *Secrets of Multilevel Marketing*

In the last chapter we discussed the reasons behind MLM's failures and therefore highlighted some factors that are essential to consider. Apart from that, what MLM companies can do to get the most out of their multi-level marketing campaign. Is there any MLM secret to success? How can we differentiate ourselves from the thousands of competitors already in the market? How can we offer more? Here are some MLM secrets to success:

Support, support and more support:

You have to stay in the back of your team. Never let your MLM team survive on its own. Keep them up to date and educate them about the product, the company and current market trends and technologies. Remember that the survival and success of your team ensures the survival of your company.

Offer something extra

Good companies always offer a little more to earn the trust and loyalty of their employees. Always try to develop relationships with your team. Identify their problems and help them solve them. Also some extra bonuses that are offered to them, for example, at Christmas, or that can send them training to improve their marketing skills in the expenses of the company, are strategies that can foster goodwill and loyalty in their team.

Provide free promotional tools:

Offering free promotional tools will help you generate more sales. The benefits you offer can bring you prospects, for example, offering free products or services that may include free products or services. Remarkable tactics, especially if you are offering health products or cosmetic products. You receive gifts, including free products and services.

Encourage teamwork:

Multilevel marketing is based on teamwork and relationship building. It is also beneficial for a company to use techniques that encourage teamwork among its distributors' network. You can do this by organizing seminars at regular intervals, involving team members through online chat rooms and other social networks where people can meet and learn from each other.

Develop an appropriate attitude

All MLM marketers must learn the secret of developing a proper attitude while conducting their business, especially when you are in the MLM online business. Since you are not in direct contact with your customer, your attitude should be such that it attracts your prospect. Respect your prospects and be honest, sincere and polite at all times. Communicate with your potential buyers in a respectful manner. One good thing to know is that people follow you, once they like you and buy from you.

Therefore, by incorporating these secrets you can offer something more to your people and your customers and thus reap the long-term benefits.

Conclusion: Summary

Multilevel marketing is an asset for any company that wants to penetrate the market and generate profits. Every business dreams of making more sales in order to make a profit. By incorporating MLM techniques companies can easily achieve their goals, but again it is important to remember that there are no shortcuts. Consistency, hard work and effort are the requirements for success.

Although MLM is usually seen as a scam or illegal, it is not illegal. It's completely legal. Beware, however, of the fraudulent practices that less legitimate companies often employ in the course of their business. Also genuine MLM companies must strictly follow the legal guidelines and ethical means of the employees' practices that not only ensure the success, but also the long-term persistence of the company.

The other dimension of MLM is its extreme flexibility which makes it possible for many people around it to get involved in the business and generate money at their own pace. One thing every multi-level marketer must understand is that it's not a miracle and it takes time and effort to ultimately succeed, so never get angry about initial failures and never give up quickly. Go ahead and keep working hard and you won't be far from success and reaping big incomes.

Now yes, I wish you the best in your results, and remember, everything is practical; theory without action is of no use to you.

A big hug, your friend, Gaston!

By the way, when you achieve your results little by little, I highly recommend you, if you want to learn much more about methods of making money, my book, on "HOW TO MAKE MONEY WITH YOUR BLOG IN 2019", is a book that I am sure will help you a lot on your way to "financial freedom". Without further ado, you can find it in the Amazon search engine, like: "How to earn money with your blog in 2019" or looking for my name, like: "Gaston Echevarria"... Once again I wish you success in your results!